Money Machine

A Quick & Easy Beginner's All-Ages Guide to Stock Market Investing & Building Passive Income

Without the Risk of Trial & Error

Sensei Paul David

COPYRIGHT PAGE

Title: Subtitle, by Sensei Paul David,
Copyright © 2020.

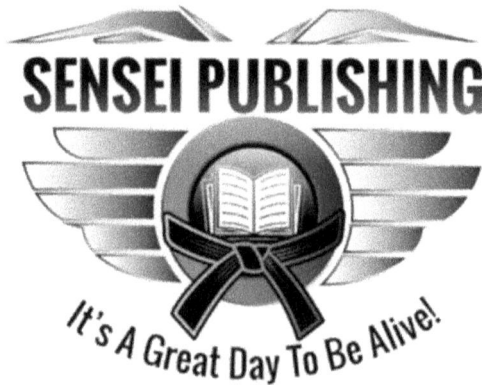

SENSEI PUBLISHING

It's A Great Day To Be Alive!

www.senseipublishing.com

@senseipublishing
senseipublishing

Check Out Another Book in This Series Visit:

www.amazon.com/author/senseipauldavid

Or

Search Amazon.com #senseipublishing

senseiselfdevelopment.senseipublishing.com

Get Our FREE Books Today!

Click & Share the Links Below

FREE Kids Books
lifeofbailey.senseipublishing.com
kidsonearth.senseipublishing.com

FREE Self-Development Book for Every Family
senseiselfdevelopment.senseipublishing.com

Join Our Publishing Journey!

If you would like to receive FUTURE FREE BOOKS and get to know us better, please click www.senseipublishing.com and join our newsletter by entering your email address in the pop-up box.

Follow Our Blog:
senseipauldavid.ca

Follow/Like/Subscribe: Facebook, Instagram, YouTube: @senseipublishing

Scan the QR Code with your phone or tablet
to follow us on social media: Like / Subscribe / Follow

Table of Contents

Foreword

Sensei Paul David

Sensei Paul David gained much of his financial knowledge working as a Financial Services Project Manager for State Street Global Bank for seven years. He has also gained personal experience and financial expertise through his experience with investing for more than a decade. In this book, Sensei Paul takes the wealth of financial and investment knowledge he has gained in his professional and personal life, through his own experience and learning from the greats, to offer the reader a simplified version of the seemingly complex investment concepts such as compounding and market fluctuations. He teaches the reader how to model stock picks after famous experts, without having to be an expert yourself. Sensei David's method is to teach the reader how to transform the uncertainty they have about risk into a curiosity to learn and form the habits necessary for continuous financial self-education.

I Learned the Hard Way So You Don't Have To!

In my early 20's I worked very hard to aggressively save my money for years. I spent a while investing in mutual funds, at this point in my life, until I realized how fees were eating away at my wealth and disavowed mutual funds forever. In my efforts to increase my wealth through investing, I took the advice my father gave me to invest all of my savings into a house, fix that house up, and then rent it to build equity. At that point I didn't know anything about investing in property and believed that my father would take the reins, advising me throughout the process. I followed his advice without question. I spent over a year searching for a home to purchase, looking at over 80 homes in various cities, learning as much as I could in the process.

At 27 I finally found the home that seemed perfect. It was a fixer-upper bungalow in a strange part of a far-away suburb. From the outside, the house was an all-brick gem. It was settled in a smaller subdivision near a local General Motors plant. In my naïveté, I thought this was the perfect location, in a quaint area, near a seemingly ample supply of qualified and interested renters. I dedicated all of my free time I could find outside of my fulltime job (3 cities away) to renovating the home. I renovated the main floor moderately and focused most of my energy fixing up the basement. I created a beautiful, comfortable 2-family dwelling with zero experience. With only my wit, my mother, my friends, and unimaginable stress – covered by smiles – I managed this feat with almost no investment in renovations.

After only one year, I realized my renters had declared war on each other. A landlord's worst nightmare had come true. My tenants were using my home as a battleground to exact revenge on another in their feud. There was a kitchen fire, income cheques were stolen from, and by both families (this was before direct deposit was the norm), garbage was strewn all over the property and both families refused to pay rent. Having no money, I had to learn quickly how to act as my own lawyer. I took both families to small claims court to force them to pay what they owed me. I was also forced to call the marshal to have both families removed from the property so I could begin repairs. I had won both battles, but I was far from a celebratory mood. To top off this horrific experience, one day while I was cleaning the now empty house, I found that the tenants had made threats against me and I was forced to call 911. This whole experience took so much out of me that my family doctor recommended I go on leave from work to get my life in order and I took her advice.

It took another full year to sell the house, after both families were removed, and the property was repaired. At the end of the day, I had lost 3 years of my life, all of my investment, and my confidence. It took me a long time to recover emotionally and financially from this experience, but I decided not to be defeated. I picked myself up and learned another way to invest. I learned how to make passive income without the anxiety of an "all or nothing" approach like what my father had advised. I realized that what my father had taught me was not the way for me. At this point in my life, I now know more than my father (may he rest in peace) could have ever taught me about wealth management. An old adage says "you teach the business you know" and my experience has proven this true.

Now, after personal experience, gained from bad and good investments, self-teaching, and my career, I am here to offer to teach any who are genuinely curious (and understandably cautious – as I was when I was a financial novice) the business I know (and am continually learning). This book is written to speak to beginners, understanding that this is a new territory for you to explore. Luckily, the pattern of success in this area leaves clues. It is these clues that I have tested and will share with you in this book. My hope is that you will take this knowledge and put it into action in your life. The most successful investors on the planet all believe that there's no time to waste when it comes to getting started on investing, so let's begin!

What This Book Gives the Reader

This book promises to provide the reader with four things:

1. A single resource for a streamlined synopsis from many of the most successful investment books and using the most successful investors' strategies.

2. A path to action, which includes the mindset and broker tools you need to consider, and advice on how to hold onto more money by avoiding long-term fees.

3. A simple resource guide written in plain English to support and coach you every step of the way, whenever you need advice or insight.

4. A FREE specialized bonus guided meditation to recap the finer points of this book in a faster and easier way than ever before.

Introduction

"An investment in knowledge pays the best interest."
Benjamin Franklin

Purpose & Value of This Book

This book is designed to work as a reference and guide to provide you with insights from the best investors on earth, so that you can create and implement an investment strategy that will "make money work for you" (in the words of Robert Kiyosaki). This book is intended for those who have never invested, as well as those who are already dabbling in the market.

This book will help you cultivate a wealth-focused, financially smart mindset and will teach you tips, tricks, and skills that you can use to expertly manage your money and create a "money machine" that works 24/7, 365 days a year, to build wealth for you and your legacy.

The "money machine" metaphor refers to a wealth-producing system that works passively and is built from a broad portfolio of held investments that compound and produce a stream of income.

This book leverages and condenses the insights and lessons from giants in wealth production and financial guidance. This labour-unintensive guide combines and condenses this sage advice into one pithy guide, saving you time, money, and mental energy, while providing you access to the lessons of top earners and teachers in investment and money-making.

My story

To quote a well-known US song, "I wish I knew what I know now when I was younger." Ten years ago, when I began investing, knowing the information I will provide to you in this book, would have saved me a lot of energy and disappointment. I may not have fallen into the same financial pitfalls, specifically around my investment property, had I known then what I know now.

That is the goal of this book: to share the wisdom I have gained through my own experience investing, as well as the knowledge I gained working as a project manager for the global US Institutional Bank at State Street, combined with the wisdom of other financial giants, to provide a condensed, comprehensible, and effective guide to investment and money-making. This book will give you insider access to the information, habits, and strategies that I learned and tested in my work in the world of investments.

I will always be a student in this area—though, as many of the greatest financial thinkers would seem to agree, financial education is always an ongoing process. However, this does not mean that I am not equipped to also be a teacher. I am passionate about distilling what I've learned in my research and practice, to inspire people of all ages across the world to cultivate an appetite for financial knowledge and to use this knowledge to take the leap into the realization of their wealth-production potential. I want others to become as excited as I am to be a lifelong learner in personal money management and to continue to pay this information forward.

The key benefit of this book lies in the pool of knowledge from which its lessons are drawn. This book provides a condensed and simplified collection of knowledge, advice, and techniques from financial experts across a range of disciplines. This book brings together, and puts on a silver platter for you, the wisdom of the most successful investment experts, including:

- Jack Bogel
- Benjamin Graham
- Peter Lynch
- Robert Kiyosaki
- Warren Buffett
- Ray Dalio
- Carl Icahn

This book will serve people of all ages and circumstances who want to access and implement the most secure, simple, economical, effective, enjoyable strategies and practices for "making your money work for you." This guide will provide you with the groundwork you need to take hold of your financial future and build your net worth. This guide will help you recognize and seize control over your fears and follies, giving you a guide to mimic the habits of financial experts.

DISCLAIMER:

I am not a financial advisor. While I have gained financial knowledge and know-how through my own experience and self-teaching, I am not a professional expert. The information and tips included in this guide are meant as advice based upon my own experience and are not a guarantee of financial success.

This book contains affiliate links. If you use these links to buy something, we may earn a commission. Thanks

Thank You from The Author: Sensei Paul David

Before we dive in, I'd like to thank you for picking up this book. Your time is valuable, and I know there are many other similar books out there, but you chose to invest in mine, and that means everything to me.

Now that you're here, and if you stick with me, I promise to make our time together valuable and worthwhile.

In the pages ahead, you will find some areas of information and practices more helpful than others - and that's great because as you apply what works best for you. You will benefit from an exciting transformation of character and knowledge. Enjoy!

Chapter 1: Introduction

"Don't gamble. Take all your savings and buy some good stock and hold it until it goes up, then sell it. If it doesn't go up, don't buy it."

Will Rogers

1.1 What is Money?

Money is the representation of the exchange in value. For consumers, value means the quality of a product or service—for example, the amount of labour and/or time required to make it, the quality of materials used, or the rarity or desirability of the product or service. This is why higher quality objects, that are more highly sought after, cost more money. For business owners, value is the ability to help solve or prevent problems as quickly, easily, and economically as possible. For example, it is the ability to repair failing equipment, technology, or systems. It is also the ability to invest in new properties, or equipment or employees of a business, to keep pace with demand.

1.2 What is Investing?

Investing is a venture—often, an adventure—in helping many types of companies add value to many customers.

When you invest in various companies, you get to ride

'piggyback' on these companies' long term successes, to receive little gifts of money, that you give to more companies, to receive more and more gifts of money, over and over again. You become part of a community of financially educated people and can share your future experiences and learnings with others, to help them learn about investing as well.

1.3 Why Is This Book Important?

In investing, you'll want to first understand the following:

- Learn to manage your money yourself to cut down on the fees and taxes you pay to advisors.
- Achieve financial literacy and learn to feel comfortable dealing

with your finances and making financial decisions.

- Gain insight into different types of income—earned, portfolio, and passive—and how they are taxed.
- Learn why passive income is important.

This book will help you get started with these topics, and more, to help you best manage your portfolio and overall finances.

Chapter 2. Work on Your Investment Attitude

Humans are not rational creatures. Our decisions are often driven by emotions and it takes effort to learn how to make good decisions. This chapter discusses ways to invest more rationally and improve your "investment attitude."

Chapter 2.1: Control Your Money Mindset

"The market serves, it does not instruct!" (Warren Buffett)

Why Invest?

There are four key reasons to begin investing. First, market growth is steady over time. This may seem counterintuitive given that almost everyone alive today has seen at least one, maybe as many as three recessions and even depression. However, in the long run, increases in overall market value are as dependable as taxation. While the market may ebb and flow, over the course of years and more so over decades, if you invest intelligently, you will see a return.

Second, throughout each year you give money away without a return, you should be getting some back for yourself. With every paycheck, you hand a portion of your money away in taxes, likely with a grumble, but nonetheless, you do it without a fight. Why not hand a portion of your money to your future self by investing? In this way regularly putting money into investments is a sort of self-taxation, but (if done correctly) one in which you will see that money come back—and then some.

Third, you work for your money and, in turn, the owners or CEOs of that business profit in the process. Why not run your own investment business and return a profit for yourself? Investing is basically owning a business in which your investments are your employees, working by themselves, with your financial foundation, to produce profit for you. Get your money to work for you instead of working for your money—this is the wealth mentality.

Fourth and finally, you should invest because of the potential to earn significant profits from dividends. Although there are stocks that do not offer dividends, most stocks return dividends on a quarterly basis (every three months) and some offer an annual or monthly dividend.

The only way to make your money work for you is to add massive value by supporting and owning a piece of other businesses, thus piggybacking on their gains and cutting your losses while you make money—increasing a variety of multiple dividend returns for the rest of your life, 24 hours a day, 365 days a year.

What Are Dividends?

Dividends are a distribution of a company's earnings to shareholders. Dividends are measured in terms of their yield— that is, how much money you get. They are typically distributed as a small percentage of the overall stock's value (typically, about 2-3%, but some dividend stocks can offer closer to a 6% yield), once or several times a year. Essentially, dividends are icing on the cake: extra (free) money on top of your increase in a portfolio's worth when stock values eventually rise.

How Should You Invest: Mindset?

To quote Warren Buffet's statement that is as valuable as it is short:

"Think independently." There is no one best way to invest—though don't confuse this with saying that there is no wrong, because there are plenty. However, you have to focus on finding the best way to invest intelligently, and relatively securely, in a way that works for your income level, goals, principles, and lifestyle.

That being said, *every* investment strategy should be comprehensive, regardless of what you invest in and how much you invest. You need to be in the mindset of carefully watching where your money is going and what you are getting in returns. As the saying goes, "Take care of the pennies and the dollars will take care of themselves."

To do this, you must view your role as a part-owner of what you invest in. This includes the realization that you cannot control consumer behaviour (the market). While you can guarantee that over time the market will grow in value, no one can predict what will happen with the market, or when, at any particular point in time. Any expert who claims to be able to predict exact market behaviour at a specific time is either lying or delusional. The only guarantee is that without investing you will not receive a return.

How Should You Invest: Money?

In order for your money to work as a profitable business, you must set aside a portion of your income that is earmarked for investment, and this purpose must be non-negotiable, no matter what. You must treat your investment funding with the same sense of necessity that you treat paying rent or taxes or buying groceries.

This is the most important rule of building your money machine. Without putting your money into investments, you can never tap the power of compounding interest returns -- what Albert Einstein has called "the eighth wonder of the world," as he says, "He who understands it, earns it; he who doesn't, pays it.".

Becoming an expert in personal finance will not only give you the power of knowledge, but it will save you a significant amount of money,

money that you can turn into investments, thus redoubling the financial value of handling your own finances and investments. Handling your own finances and investments not only renders you in complete control of your financial destiny, but it will save you from the fees—stated and hidden—associated with paying a financial advisor, an expense that can add up significantly over the years.

How Should You Invest: Portfolio?

Sometimes the best way to explain something is through analogy. Your portfolio is like a litter of puppies. Stick with me here, imagine you have a litter of puppies. Each puppy is different from the others, some grow faster than others, some require more food than others, but they all grow. Further, if you play your cards right and make intelligent choices with your behaviour, you can raise them to aid you however you need.

Your stock portfolio is like this litter of puppies, in that each instrument in your portfolio is unique, requiring different amounts of "sustenance" (funding) and growing at different rates. However, as you keep "feeding" these instruments with funding, as time passes, your investments will naturally grow bigger and stronger. These investments will come to serve and protect you, your home, and your legacy from harm, like a pack of guard dogs.

"I work to learn how to make money with money. I don't work for money, money works for me."
Robert Kiyosaki

Chapter 2.2: Understand & Control Your Equity Emotions

Almost everyone learns to feel an emotional attachment to their money. This makes perfect sense. Money is, after all, a representation of value. For the worker, their income is the representation of the arduous work that they put in to earn that money. In an immediate sense, money represents hours of labour and stress. However, this is only the sole representation of money for those who don't understand the power of investing. For those who do, money also represents the potential for exponentiated wealth.

Part of the emotional fear of parting with money for investment, comes from misinformation or misunderstanding (or downright lack of information) from school, families, friends -- many if not most people do not have a proper financial education. Your avoidance of investing your money needs to stop here. You need to let go of the emotional attachment and act logically and intelligently to use the market, which means using some of your income in the market, to make your money make money.

The key to overcoming this fear, and the key to significant financial growth in the market, is to remember that you are playing the long (waiting) game. Building your financial wealth will not happen overnight in the sense that you will likely not wake up tomorrow and be a millionaire, unless you get a sizable inheritance.

However, it can happen while you sleep, if you invest intelligently and automate your investments.

The most important thing to remember is to be patient and know that while short-term downfalls (crashes) may occur, overall, the market is stable and day-to-day or month-to-month profit and loss do not determine income in the long run. This is not to say that you will not see growth in the short term, but it is to say that you need to be ready to persist despite what seem like immediate setbacks or stagnations.

The goal is to focus on building a money machine that will make you money "while you sleep" (automatically) and that will return significant long-term income (not cash in your pocket right away). Reassure yourself you are taking control and leveraging your money while you sleep. Approximately 30% of your life is spent sleeping, so if you live to be 90 and never invested you would have wasted 30 years of time you could have been making returns. Keep Telling yourself this is a slow process especially at first— and that's okay.

Chapter 2.3: Adopt & Maintain a Relaxed and Long-Term Discipline

Go Ultra-Long

The key to investing is to be in it for the long haul. One thing that can help you with your mindset is understanding compounding for both fees and dividend yield returns.

It can be useful to automate your contributions any way you can—to "set it and forget it" to help keep your mind off the ups and downs of the market. Most financial websites allow you to make recurring contributions on a weekly, monthly, or even annual basis. You will need to connect your financial brokerage account with your bank account to be able to do this, so make sure you have enough money each time the automatic contribution is taken out.

Understand Compound Interest and The Effects of Time on Investing in General

You may want to assess your contributions in terms of your age. Young people in their 20s and 30s often are working entry-level jobs and can't afford to make a lot of contributions, but because of compounding, any amount you invest could be greatly magnified, as it will be accruing interest over a longer period. People in their 40s and above may have more money, due to their longer time in the job market and more experienced, higher-paying jobs, but will have less time for the interest to accrue, so it may be possible to contribute more. So you will want to take age into account in coming up with an investment strategy.

Understand compounding for both fees and dividend yield returns.

When it comes to fees, they add up over the years and can impede the growth of your Money Machine. The below graph is an illustrative example, depicting the loss in return that can occur with a compounding fee rate of just 2%.

Costs can eat away at your investments

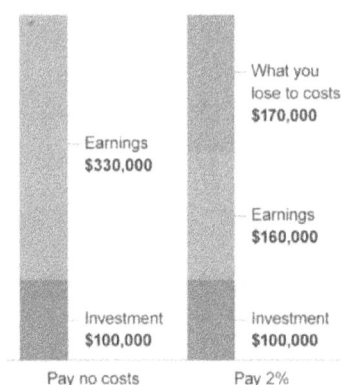

What you
lose to costs
$170,000

Earnings
$330,000

Earnings
$160,000

Investment
$100,000

Investment
$100,000

Pay no costs   Pay 2%

This hypothetical illustration doesn't represent any particular investment nor does it account for inflation. "What you lose to costs" represents both the amount paid in expenses as well as the "opportunity costs"—the amount you lose because the costs you paid are no longer invested. There may be other material differences between investment products that must be considered prior to investing. Numbers are rounded.

(Source: Vanguard "The Impact of Investment Costs")

On the other hand, compounding is your friend when it comes to dividend investing. Take the following example. Assume, for a given period of time, that the stock price remains relatively stable. You buy the stock, knowing that it has a relatively stable price and gives a good dividend (Tip: utilities stocks can be great for this). Then, you receive a dividend. The value of your investment is now 103% of its initial value. When another dividend rolls around, you get another 3% of your 103% back—which is an additional 3.09%. So, after two rounds of a 3% dividend, your investment is now 106.09% of its original value.

Higher dividend rates produce exponentially higher growth in returns. If your dividend yield is 5% then the first dividend increases that to 105%, with the second 5% dividend increasing your investment value to 110.25%. This increase is known as the <u>dividend growth rate</u>, and the higher the dividend growth rate, the better.

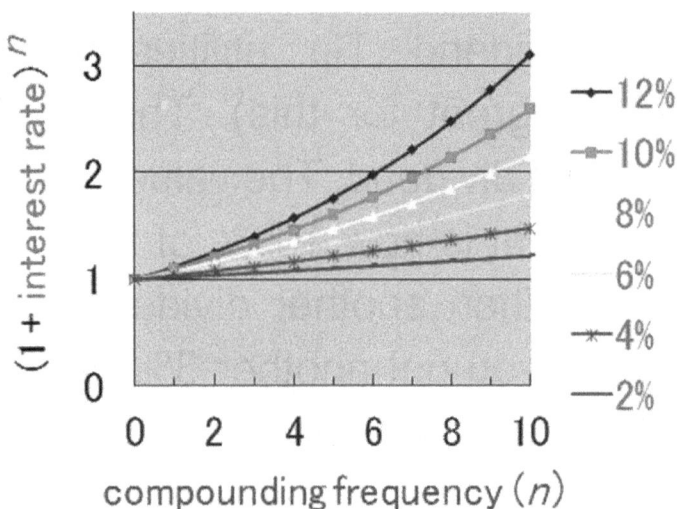

As the above graph illustrates, a higher compound interest rate helps you build your Money Machine more rapidly. (Source: <u>Wikipedia</u>)

You can think of compound interest as a small snowball that eventually collects enough snow to become a larger snowball. Compound interest applied to long term investing builds momentum for your portfolio and helps ensure excellent returns. Time is your friend in the compound investing game. With this type of investing, you can invest, and continuously learn and optimize. A few years later, you will find that your money machine has improved mainly by itself.

Make investing a required expense.

As discussed above, you have to pay taxes every year, so why not pay yourself and make it a non-negotiable aspect of your finances? The advantage is that, unlike taxes, in investing, you get to keep the money for yourself.

The challenge here is to figure out a system that works for you. The 50/30/20 rule can be helpful here— use 50% of your after-tax pay on things you need, 30% on things you want, and 20% on savings.

Chapter 2.4: Risks to Avoid

Don't act on your instincts.

Don't give up, sell, or buy, without thinking ahead. This is also known as consequential thinking. What would be the benefit of your desired actions? What would be the disadvantages? Think it through before you make a decision.

Figure out how much you'll make when you sell (make sure to take into account any taxes or fees), including long-term scenarios in which you could make more by staying in the market. Work out these scenarios in your head before you buy, sell, or give up.

It's important to remember that, sometimes, the market reacts to "hype" or the latest news. These downturns are typically temporary and driven by emotional thinking which leads to sell-offs. In the long term, the market recovers from such minute corrections. Learn to take measured, strategic actions rather than emotional, drastic actions in the investment world.

Don't ignore hidden fees.

Ask questions. Don't pay more than you need to. Fees slowly compound and slow the growth of your wealth. Here are a few examples:

A 1% fee over 1 year leaves you with 99%. Over 10 years, you will be left with just over 90% of your original investment.

1% fees over 10 years equal over 10% in lost growth.

2% fees over 10 years equal over 18% in lost growth.

3% fees over 10 years equal over 26% in lost growth.

Here, I'm just walking you through the math in a hypothetical scenario. Here's a more concrete real-world example:

Using the SEC graph below, we can see how seemingly minor increases in fee rates can drastically erode your take-home from investments over time.

With an initial investment of $100,000 and a .5% annual fee, you will see $10,000 less in returns over 20 years compared to a .25% annual fee. When the fee doubles to 1%, this loss triples to $30,000 after 20 years.

Portfolio Value From Investing $100,000 Over 20 Years

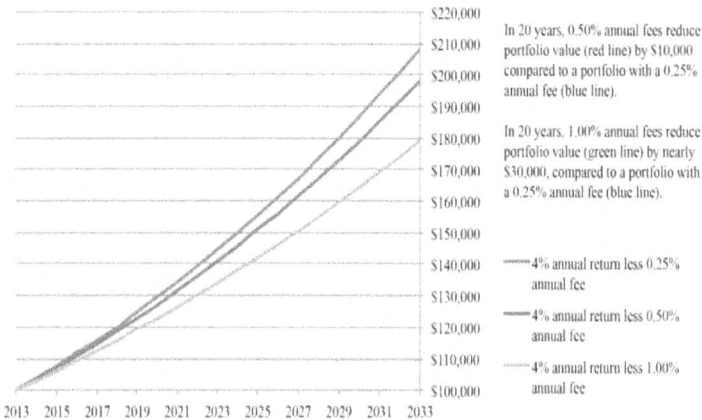

In 20 years, 0.50% annual fees reduce portfolio value (red line) by $10,000 compared to a portfolio with a 0.25% annual fee (blue line).

In 20 years, 1.00% annual fees reduce portfolio value (green line) by nearly $30,000, compared to a portfolio with a 0.25% annual fee (blue line).

——— 4% annual return less 0.25% annual fee

——— 4% annual return less 0.50% annual fee

——— 4% annual return less 1.00% annual fee

(Source: SEC "Investor Bulletin: How Fees and Expenses Affect Your Investment Portfolio")

Don't ignore tax rules.

Educate yourself regarding your government's tax laws and how they pertain to affecting your investments when you withdraw funds, when you leave funds, and when you reinvest. Write down your questions and call your revenue agency and speak to an expert. Write down their answers!

Invest in yourself.

Maximize your investment in yourself by minimizing your losses to fees. This is the key to lowering and eliminating fees.

Mutual funds can bring good returns but have high fees. On the other hand, cash accounts, like a bank savings account, can underperform over time, compared to stocks.

Fees make a difference. As a kid in the 1980s in Canada, I remember that some people would rent a stationary phone for a low monthly fee, and some people would buy a stationary phone for a noticeable, but not outrageously high, one-time fee. The people who bought the phone made an investment and didn't continue to pay for it. But the people who rented the phone were paying a pernicious fee for years, never noticing the hundreds and thousands of dollars given away over many years—dollars that could have been slowly compounded to help, instead of unknowingly eating away at their savings over the years.

Invest in yourself and you'll see the metaphorical and literal dividends materialize.

Understand the nature of the stock market.

The stock market can be viewed as analogous to the weather and seasons. Weather is short-term and unpredictable, while seasons are longer-term and approximately predictable. The same goes for the stock market. Changes happen due to news and hype, which are in the short-term. The longer-term trends are more predictable and operate in an approximate 10-year cycle.

A "bull market" is a market that is expected to rise, increasing the value of investments. On the other hand, a "bear" market is a market that decreases the value of investments 20% or more from recent highs, causing pessimism for others about the future. Historically, there's roughly an approximate 10-year cycle of a bull market, followed by an approximate 2 years of a bear market.

In a bear market, stocks are down, and dividend yields increase (which pay you more money). Bear markets are actually a great time to buy because most or all the positions (stocks) go on sale—and a lucky time to get started in investing. However, time in the market, beats timing the market, ultimately— meaning that any time is a great time to start investing.

In a bull market, when stocks show a pattern of improvement, dividend yields decrease (which pay you less money). Bear markets are a great time for investors—assuming the investments are reliable (blue chip) stocks that show many years of never having missed a dividend distribution (or payout). This can be easily checked online nowadays.

Basis points are a common measurement unit for interest rates. One basis point is the equivalent of 1/100th of 1%, as <u>Investopedia</u> defines it. A 1% change, therefore, is 100 basis points.

Chapter 2.5: Positions to Invest in and their Nature

When you buy an investment, you can say you have taken a position in it, whether it is a company, property, fund, or another type of investment. When considering positions to invest in, you should consider all the different possibilities for the best outcomes. Here are a few different positions:

- **Vanguard Index funds** were founded by finance guru Jack Bogle in the 1970s. They are more expensive and do not pay out as much but tend to be more reliable. Index funds are designed to mirror a market index, so you end up becoming an owner in the market.
- **Real Estate Investment Trusts or REITs** include property or mortgage. This can include apartments, office buildings, and retail spaces.
- **Exchange-Traded Funds or ETFs** are pre-picked baskets of

funds, but they won't make you rich.

- **Individual stocks** may make you more money, but they may or may not survive a bear market, so you need to do your research.

Chapter 3. Tools and Resources.

"A successful man is one who can lay a firm foundation with the bricks others have thrown at him."
David Brinkley

Chapter 3.1: Websites to Help You Get Started Investing

Many large banks allow you to open investment brokerage accounts and offer to buy and to sell with little to no commissions or fees. However, there are also smaller, independent self-serve brokers that are alternatives to those offered by large banks. I prefer these smaller brokers because they are among the most user-friendly investment apps, both in terms of their interface and customer support. They are also more effective and efficient than many other investment tools, including traditional banks. The interface for these websites also appears more simple and the customer support element is faster and more effective to my mind.

- <u>Questrade</u>
- <u>Wealthsimple</u>
- <u>Robinhood</u>

You must do your own comparative research and make your own decision about which broker to use—and stick to that decision. However, I will offer a brief overview of each of these platforms to help you get started in your comparison.

Questrade

What is Questrade?

Questrade is a mobile and desktop investment and trading platform for Canadian residents offering access to various investment products and portfolio management options at low fees.

What Can You Do on Questrade?

Questrade offers a platform for savings, investment, and trading in an array of products and markets so that you can broaden your portfolio and leverage your investments.

The Questrade platform offers you the ability to invest in:

· Stocks (long and short)

- Options (simple and multi-leg)
- Bonds (through a live broker)
- Exchange-Traded Funds (EFTs)
- Mutual Funds
- Contracts for Difference (CFDs) (requires additional platform IQ Edge)
- Forex (requires additional platform IQ Edge)

Questrade also offers savings and investment options:

- Tax-Free Savings Accounts (TFSAs)
- Registered Retirement Savings Plans (RRSPs)
- Margin Accounts for US & CDN positions
- Guaranteed Investment Certificates (GICs)

- International Equities
- Initial Public Offerings (IPOs)
- Precious Metal Purchases

Questrade offers free snapshots of basic market information, or, for an additional fee, live-streamed market updates, from top market sources, such as NYSE and NASDAQ. This simplified information snapshot shows your balances, buying power, positions, margin balances, and profit and loss. You can customize which information you are shown to make your trading decisions more efficient.

How Easy is Questrade to Use?

Questrade is designed to facilitate the investment process, offering an intuitive and simplified platform that functions the same whether you are using it on your computer or a smart device.

Wealthsimple

What is Wealthsimple?

Wealthsimple is a desktop and mobile investment and saving platform for Canadian, US, and UK residents providing algorithm-based automated portfolio management and saving services at low fees with a $0 minimum opening balance.

What Can You Do with Wealthsimple?

The Wealthsimple platform facilitates financial goal achievement by employing an algorithm, based on Modern Portfolio Theory, calculated using your responses to a questionnaire concerning:

- financial goals
- time-frame
- risk tolerance
- investment experience
- level of investment knowledge

The Wealthsimple portfolio building and management algorithm uses generic buy and hold strategies, is populated by 8-10 well-founded investment instruments, and employs tried and true market strategies including:

- diversification of asset classes
- passive buy and hold investing
- dividend reinvestment
- risk scoring
- your feedback

However, you do have some basic control over your portfolio construction. You can choose from socially conscious (e.g. eco-friendly) portfolios and Halal accounts. You can also change the proportion of your funding devoted to each instrument.

The Wealthsimple website shows your key account features and allows you to review your transactions and investment performance statistics based upon movement toward each of your financial goals. Further, Wealthsimple live representatives can be reached by phone or email (though no live chat). You can speak with a live financial advisor upon request and you can hold unlimited financial planning sessions as a member (you are allowed one session as a non-member).

Finally, Wealthsimple also provides numerous easy-to-use financial and investment education tools, including a thorough "Investing 101" glossary, a comprehensive investment FAQ page, covering common questions and concerns, and monthly blogs and magazine issues which include numerous financial and investing "How-To" discussions.

How Easy is Wealthsimple to Use?

Wealthsimple makes smart investing and saving a no-brainer. Using an algorithm that populates your portfolio with ETFs, mutual funds, or a combination (depending upon which region you live in) and determines the proportion of funds towards each, to maximize your potential to reach your financial goals, while minimizing your risk of loss. The portfolio is automatically compiled by Wealthsimple based upon your answers to their profile-building questionnaire and your selections in the pool of potential financial goals.

The Wealthsimple algorithm takes the guesswork out of investing by automatically rebalancing your portfolio based upon your progress toward your goals and following deposits, withdrawals, and changes in asset values or risk score. Wealthsimple also automatically determines the nature of your portfolio as conservative, balances, or growth-focused based upon your profile and goals.

Transfers are as easy as a few clicks of your mouse. You can transfer taxable or retirement accounts to start your Wealthsimple account, or you can deposit new funds. The website is mobile-ready and easy to read and navigate.

Robinhood

What is Robinhood?

Robinhood is a mobile investment and trading platform, available as a mobile device application or traditional website. It is designed for the most novice of investors. Robinhood is noted for its simplicity, low deposit requirements (no minimum), and low stock purchase requirements (you can purchase partial shares).

What Can You Do with Robinhood?

Robinhood's key selling points are that it allows you to invest in stocks—including partial stocks – and trade in cryptocurrency with no minimum investment requirements and no trading cost. The key to the Robinhood app is its simplicity and lack of minimum funding requirements (i.e. no minimum deposit). However, because the focus of Robinhood is on simplicity, there are few if any ways to customize your profile.

How Easy is Robinhood to Use?

Robinhood is noted as one of the most user-friendly and therefore simple investment applications to use. It should be noted that some of this hyper-simplicity means that this tool does not provide the same depth of information or customization that other investment apps or websites offer. However, for the novice investor, especially the novice investor who is seeking to start small (i.e. purchasing partial shares), the Robinhood app and website is one of the simplest ways to get your feet wet in investing.

Advantages and Disadvantages of Online Brokerage Firms

In Canada, we have Wealthsimple and Questrade. Wealth simple is highly automated, but there's less opportunity for learning because of the automation. Questrade is more manual and has great customer service for learning as you go— understanding taxes, fees, products and accounts. In the United States, apps like Robinhood are also available. These apps make it easy to invest from the convenience of your smartphone.

I prefer a manual self-learning approach and I use Questrade for that reason.

Chapter 3.2: Common Sense Advice for Picking Positions

Picking positions takes some effort and thought. It's a good idea to create a requirements checklist for identifying positions that meet your standards.

Here are some tips for creating such a checklist:

- Think long-term. Ask yourself, *what will help take care of me when I'm too old to work?*
- Do your research. Google what the company or fund does; its holdings; and its history, both in terms of performance and in terms of ventures.
- Check out the dividend payout. Examine dividend yield and payout history.
- Remember other indicators of success such as market cap and price—both over the last year and throughout a company's lifetime.

Once you've figured out your positions over the span of a few days, execute your trades. Time is of the essence of investing!

Chapter 3.3: Practical Tips for Getting Started

Here's some of my advice as a lifelong student investor:

- I believe time in the market beats timing the market. Don't try to time the market, just get started the best way you can with what you can afford at first.
- Expect fluctuations in unrealized value in the total value of your portfolio. This is normal. Hold on to what you have, and build upon it by regularly contributing to your portfolio and making consistent investments. Make sure to reinvest dividends right away— many brokers have the option to automatically reinvest dividends

for you in what is called a DRIP (Dividend Reinvestment Program). I prefer not to use a DRIP but to manually allocate my funds based on stock price and yield weekly.

Chapter 4: Basic Strategies

"It takes as much energy
to wish as it does to plan."
Eleanor Roosevelt

Chapter 4.1 Diversify your investments

Diversifying your investments means not putting all your eggs in one basket. When you invest in a variety of different positions, you can decrease risk by having a bunch of different "baskets" so to speak. Mitigate risk by investing in a variety of different stocks. For example, you may opt for a value investment approach with a few well-researched investments in riskier positions.

Consider, for example, investing in both NYSE and NASDAQ stocks so that if the NASDAQ hits a low, you still have some liquidity in the markets due to your other investments.

Diversification of investments is the best way to reduce risk and maximize gains.

"Keeping your money spread across many stocks and industries is the only reliable insurance against the risk of being wrong. But diversification doesn't just minimize your odds of being wrong. It also maximizes your chance of being right."—Ben Graham, *The Intelligent Investor*

Chapter 4.2: Don't Spend More than You Earn.

Analyze your monthly expenditures. When you're working on managing your finances, the most important part is to take stock of your monthly expenditures and make sure that you have the money for them. If you find yourself unable to pay the bills each month and seem to be escalating toward debt, check in with your finances.

Make a budget and see whether you can stick to it. If you cannot live within your means, you will need to cut things out of your budget or see if you can get a job that enables you to make ends meet. Making a budget and comparing it to your typical spending is a great way to stay accountable for your finances. Oftentimes, you will notice that you can cut back in some places to save money. Perhaps your shopping habit is out of control, and you are holding on to goods you can either sell or return to the store—or you just need to cut back. Maybe you've been eating too much takeout and delivery from local restaurants when you could just cook at home. Whatever your spending patterns are, figure them out—and learn from them to come up with a budget that works for you.

Chapter 4.3: Devote a certain amount of money per month to building your money machine.

Once you check in with your finances, as discussed in Chapter 3.1, you can start building your money machine. By "money machine," I mean the investment portfolio that earns you passive dividend income, which you can reinvest to make your money machine grow faster. To do this, dedicate a certain amount of money per month—that you never touch— to building your money machine. Learning the keys to financial success means learning from the wisdom of those who have managed financial success.

According to *The Automatic Millionaire* ,by David Bach, those who want to be "super-rich, super-fast" should "pay themselves first" by setting aside at least 20% of their gross income. Not setting aside anything, or setting aside anything less than 5%, can set one up for being "poor" or even "dead broke."

In your journey to learn the keys to financial success, it is vital to be familiar with the greats in financial success -- to stand on the shoulders of giants, you must first know who the giants are. Jim Rohn is one of the most well-known and well-respected of these greats. He was a trail-blazing self-starter, investment and business guru, and financial mentor.

From humble beginnings as the child of Idaho farmers in mid-twentieth century, Rohn made a rapid rise to financial success and fame by his early thirties following the advice of his mentor Earl Shoaff. He has been invited to speak to audiences from high school students to Rotary Clubs, quickly expanding to paid seminars to packed audiences. Jim Rohn has also published numerous popular books and won numerous industry awards, inspiring millions with his approachable and grounded attitude to personal finance building, from an insightful human behaviour based philosophy and the mentor of world-renowned life coach Tony Robbins.

Jim Rohn suggests a fairly simple breakdown of proportions of expenditures to build a portfolio that will set you up for financial greatness which will allow you a comfortable living and still leave room for spreading the wealth so that you can build your karma while you build your wealth. He suggests devoting 70% of your income to your living expenses (bills, groceries, gas, etc.), 10% to charity, 10% to lower-risk investing, and the last 10% to higher-risk investing. This breakdown will allow you to take the necessary leaps to make meaningful gains while maintaining financial security.

However, if you can afford to devote more than 20% of your income to investing (that is if you can live off of less than 70% of your income and invest the rest), Rohn strongly suggests that you do so. Essentially, you want to devote as much of your income to investing as you reasonably can without depriving yourself of necessities and a safety net.

Especially for those who are starting out in their middle age, you will need to find ways to compound your wealth more quickly. In order to see your financial growth pay off before retirement, you will likely need to devote more than 20% of your income to invest. The more you invest, the greater your return. The more you pay into your money machine, the more you will be able to invest. The more you invest, the more your money will compound, meaning increased investments are met with exponential income growth.

Chapter 4.4: Think about Asset allocation

Dividends are usually paid out as cash payments. This means that you are free to do whatever you want with your dividend payments without having to sell your stock. Of course, you can reinvest your dividends to buy more stocks of the paying company—and this may be a wise choice if the stock is doing particularly well (more stock means more cash from dividends). However, it may be wiser yet to hold onto your dividend cash payments and use them to broaden your portfolio by buying a different stock or investment instrument. Putting your dividend cash payments in the bank to build up until the next bear market will mean that you have that much more investment power when stock prices drop (the ideal time to invest).

Chapter 4.5: Build Up Your Emergency Savings

The gold standard for savings seems to be to hold enough savings to cover six months of bills and living expenses (e.g. groceries, gas). Having this kind of savings essentially buys you six months for the economy, the market, or your current situation to stabilize (though hopefully, you would never have to use up your entire savings). Further, having sizable savings also protects you against emergencies such as home or car repairs, medical costs, or any other kind of unforeseen major expense.

Finally, having significant savings also protects you against the effects of downturns in the market (especially the shift to a bear market). As the saying goes, "time in the market beats timing the market." The market will always shift over time between a bear market and a bull market, but having savings built up means that you will be able to ride through the downturns (or life disasters or major expenses) without having to pull out of the market. If you can persevere through the bear market, you will see the reward for your perseverance when the market has an upturn and stabilizes again.

Chapter 4.6: Debt

Pay your debts and pay them on time, but don't overpay them. Meaning, after paying your monthly dues for debts, pay yourself before applying any extra income toward paying off debt. This may sound counterintuitive. You may be thinking, "Won't I lose money on interest if I take longer to pay my debts?" While this may be true, one of the common pieces of advice from successful and prominent financial experts is to pay yourself first so you can focus that money on investing. Money paid toward debt is money that you are not putting into the market. Many financial experts even say that you should pay yourself before paying *anything* else. If you want to make your money work for you, you have to make paying yourself (and investing those self-payments) a non-negotiable process. Don't think twice. Don't skip any self-payment. This is the only way to see your money grow.

Chapter 5: Voices of Wisdom

"Before you speak, listen. Before you write, think. Before you spend, earn. Before you invest, investigate. you criticize, wait. Before you pray, forgive. Before you quit, try. Before you retire, save. Before you die, give."

William A. Ward

The best way to learn sage investment advice is to read the work of the experts.

Ray Dalio

"I learned that if you work hard and creatively, you can have just about anything you want, but not everything you want. Maturity is the ability to reject good alternatives in order to pursue even better ones."

"Listening to uninformed people is worse than having no answers at all."

"In trading, you have to be defensive and aggressive at the same time."

"Don't put the expedient ahead of the strategic"

"Almost nothing can stop you from succeeding if you have a) flexibility and b) self-accountability."

Paul Tutor Jones

"I believe the very best money is made at the market turns. Everyone says you get killed trying to pick tops and bottoms and you make all your money by playing the trend in the middle. Well for twelve years I have been missing the meat in the middle but I have made a lot of money at tops and bottoms."

"If I have positions going against me, I get right out; if they are going for me, I keep them. Risk control is the most important thing in trading. If you have a losing position that is making you uncomfortable, the solution is very simple: Get out, because you can always get back in."

"The secret to being successful from a trading perspective is to have an indefatigable and an undying and unquenchable thirst for information and knowledge."

"Don't ever average losers. Decrease your trading volume when you are trading poorly; increase your volume when you are trading well. Never trade in situations where you don't have control. For example, I don't risk significant amounts of money in front of key reports, since that is gambling, not trading."

"Intellectual capital will always trump financial capital."

Peter Lynch

"If you're prepared to invest in a company, then you ought to be able to explain why in simple language that a fifth-grader could understand, and quickly enough so the fifth grader won't get bored."

"There's no shame in losing money on a stock. Everybody does it. What is shameful is to hold on to a stock, or worse, to buy more of it when the fundamentals are deteriorating."

"If you can't find any companies that you think are attractive, put your money in the bank until you discover some."

"If you don't study any companies, you have the same success buying stocks as you do in a poker game if you bet without looking at your cards."

"In the long run, a portfolio of well-chosen stocks and/or equity mutual funds will always outperform a portfolio of bonds or a money-market account. In the long run, a portfolio of poorly chosen stocks won't outperform the money left under the mattress."

Robert Kiyosaki

"The fear of being different prevents most people from seeking new ways to solve their problems."

"If you want to be rich, you need to develop your vision. You must be standing on the edge of time gazing into the future."

"Often, the more money you make the more money you spend; that's why more money doesn't make you rich – assets make you rich."

"The moment you make passive income and portfolio income a part of your life, your life will change. Those words will become flesh."

"Find the game where you can win, and then commit your life to playing it, and play to win."

Sir John Templeton

"Bull markets are born on pessimism, grown on skepticism, mature on optimism and die on euphoria. The time of maximum pessimism is the best time to buy, and the time of maximum optimism is the best time to sell."

"The only reason to sell them a stock now is to buy other, more attractive stocks. If you can't find more attractive stocks, hold on to what you have."

"The only way to avoid mistakes is not to invest—which is the biggest mistake of all."

"Forgive yourself for your errors. Don't become discouraged, and certainly don't try to recoup your losses by taking bigger risks. Instead, turn each mistake into a learning experience. Determine exactly what went wrong and how you can avoid the same mistake in the future."

Warren Buffet

"It's far better to buy a wonderful company at a fair price than a fair company at a wonderful price."

"Only buy something that you'd be perfectly happy to hold if the market shut down for 10 years."

"Wide diversification is only required when investors do not understand what they are doing."

"Look at market fluctuations as your friend rather than your enemy; profit from folly rather than participate in it."

"We've used derivatives for many, many years. I don't think derivatives are evil, per se, I think they are dangerous. ...So we use lots of things daily that are dangerous, but we generally pay some attention to how they're used. We tell the cars how fast they can go."

Mark Cuban

"One thing we can all control is effort. Put in the time to become an expert in whatever you're doing. It will give you an advantage because most people don't do this."

"It's not in the dreaming, it's in the doing."

"Creating opportunities means looking at where others are not."

"Perfectionism is the enemy of profitability."

Jack Bogel

"In recent years, annual trading in stocks — necessarily creating, by reason of the transaction costs involved, a negative value for traders — averaged some $33 trillion. But capital formation — that is, directing fresh investment capital to its highest and best uses, such as new businesses, new technology, medical breakthroughs, and modern plant and equipment for existing business — averaged some $250 billion. Put another way, speculation represented about 99.2% of the activities of our equity market system, with capital formation accounting for 0.8%."

"Investing is not nearly as difficult as it looks. Successful investing involves doing a few things right and avoiding serious mistakes."

"Time is your friend; impulse is your enemy."

"The index fund is a sensible, serviceable method for obtaining the market's rate of return with absolutely no effort and minimal expense. Index funds eliminate the risks of individual stocks, market sectors and manager selection, leaving only stock market risk."

Benjamin Graham

"An investment operation is one which, upon thorough analysis, promises safety of principal and an adequate return. Operations not meeting these requirements are speculative."

"But investing isn't about beating others at their game. It's about controlling yourself at your own game."

"People who invest make money for themselves; people who speculate make money for their brokers."

"You must thoroughly analyze a company, and the soundness of its underlying businesses, before you buy its stock; you must deliberately protect yourself against serious losses; you must aspire to "adequate," not extraordinary, performance."

"You will be much more in control if you realize how much you are not in control."

"Obvious prospects for physical growth in a business do not translate into obvious profits for investors."

Albert Einstein is reputed to have said, "**Compound interest** is the eighth wonder of the world. He who understands it earns it; he who doesn't pays it."

Chapter 6: Stand on the Shoulders of Giants

"Risk comes from not knowing what you're doing."

Warren Buffett

Money mindset books out there offer powerful advice for investors from the experts. Here are a few summaries of the best money mindset books out there.

You can find these and other books on my website here. I update this page every so often with links to my favourite books.

Rich Dad, Poor Dad By Robert Kiyosaki

In *Rich Dad, Poor Dad* Robert Kiyosaki discusses the difference in financial literacy and mentality between the rich and the poor and middle classes. Essentially, Kiyosaki holds that it is a lack of financial literacy and a mentality focused on making more money and securing that money that traps poor and middle-class individuals in the "rat race" and the cycle of debt. The poor and middle-class focus on making and keeping money through work – and securing your job as a means to this – leads them to ignore opportunities for income and financial asset growth because they are too focused on paying expenses.

The mentality of "I can't afford it" shuts off creativity, the mentality of "how can I afford it" pushes you toward action. The rich focus on learning new skills and keeping their eyes and minds open to new financial opportunities. Poor and middle-class people confuse liabilities with assets – this ends up increasing their debt. Assets make you money, liabilities cost you money. For example, it is thought, among the poor and middle classes, to be an asset because of its value, but because of derivatives, taxes, upkeep, and loss in return upon selling, houses often actually lead to more debt. Rental property on the other hand is an asset: it makes you money via rent payments. Gaining financial literacy, specifically accounting, investing, and tax law, are the keys to financial success. Don't work for money, make money work for you.

Rich Dad's Cashflow Quadrant By Robert Kiyosaki

Following from the discussion of the "rich" versus the "poor" financial/work mentality discussed in *Rich Dad, Poor Dad*, in *Cashflow Quadrant,* Kiyosaki discusses the four positions in what he calls the "cashflow quadrant" – or the four means of income: 1) employee, 2) self-employed, 3) business owner, and 4) investor. It is possible to belong to more than one quadrant, in fact, this is preferred. However, each quadrant requires particular skills, so if you are going to switch quadrants or keep one foot in multiple quadrants, you will need to possess the knowledge and skills needed for each of those quadrants. Those in the first two quadrants have the most difficulty getting rich, those in the last two quadrants have the easiest time. These quadrants are defined by four factors: 1) focus on job/income security, 2) focus on the job/financial freedom, 3) amount of personal time required for income (working hours), and 4) amount of money garnered. The employee and self-employed both place the highest value on job security, trading their time for money (they work for their money), the latter experiencing less security than the former who is shielded from disasters, such as major medical issues by employee benefits. However, neither the employee nor the self-employed experiences job or income freedom and neither is likely to make one rich. The business owner and the investor focus on job and financial freedom, garnering lots of money without having to devote considerable time to their work (their money works for them).

Secrets of the Millionaire Mindset By T. Harv Eker

T. Harv Eker's _Secrets of the Millionaire Mindset_, like the other books discussed, and as the title suggests, is a how-to guide for shifting your mindset to break old habits that keep you poor and make new ones that will help make you rich. Behaviour is learned, particularly learned from our parents. Most people learn how to get a job, what job to get, how to perceive work and holding a job, and how to save or spend our earnings from our parents and most people unconsciously replicate this learned behaviour when they are adults. The key trick to taking on the "mind of the millionaire" then is to recognize that you are in charge of how you make and spend money and to take the reins in reimagining and manifesting the mindset of the rich. In order to manifest the mindset of the rich, which allows them to make (and hold onto) their money, you must first learn to appreciate this mindset. In brief, you cannot despise a millionaire at the same time that you seek to become one. This negative mindset toward "the rich" will create a mental block and keep you from engaging with and learning from the rich. The key to gaining the "millionaire mind" is thus realizing that you are in control, taking conscious and thoughtful steps to direct your earning and spending to make more money and waste less money, and to learn to appreciate the financial wisdom that the wealthy can offer.

Think & Grow Rich By Napoleon Hill

In *Think & Grow Rich* , Napoleon Hill puts forward the simple argument that the attainment of riches derives from a single-minded and unrelenting determination to become rich. Success and failure are both end results of and driven by mindsets of success or failure. Ultimately the attainment of wealth (getting rich) is achievable if you are able to control your own mind. The best way to achieve this control over your mind is to maintain singleness of purpose and strength of desire. Hill lays out the means of achieving and maintaining that mindset throughout this book. There are four key aspects of your goal that are necessary for its achievement. First, it must be a singular goal. Second, your goal must be definite, you must know exactly what you want to achieve (exactly how much money you want to have) and exactly how you are going to achieve (what are you going to do to get that money?). Third, you must have a burning, all-consuming, desire to achieve this goal -- this desire must predominate your thoughts and energies. Fourth, you must believe that your goal will be achieved, you must visualize its achievement and build and maintain faith that it will happen. Additionally, you must be flexible. If you're not achieving your goal through the means you have developed, make a different plan. Don't give up, persistence, driven by a perpetual burning desire to achieve your goal, must be maintained. Start today, even if you don't have a plan, begin by visualizing your goal.

You Are a Badass at Making Money By Jen Sincero

In _You Are a Badass at Making Money,_ Jen Sincero takes an

arguably unconventional approach to what it means and what it takes to become "rich." Sincero, like Napoleon Hill, discusses quite often, the importance of putting your desire into the universe. However, what this ultimately means is that you have to give your mentality and energy toward achieving your financial goal and you have to visualize its manifestation and believe that it *will* happen. Unlike many other mainstream books about making money, that focus specifically on becoming a millionaire, and working the market or your career path to make this happen, Sincero offers a different definition. To be "rich" is to have enough money that you can live your best and most authentic life -- whatever that means to you. To achieve riches, you must thus take on a mindset focused upon this goal. In order to achieve this mindset, you must first understand why you want to get rich, what you would spend that money on, how you will make that money, and when you will achieve this goal. Your answers to the first two questions need to be more meaningful than the desire to swim in a pool of cash and buy a Lamborghini. You must then be willing to take a hard look at the habits you have that lead you to waste money and time (that you could use to make money). You must be willing to dive headfirst toward your goal.

The Millionaire Fastlane By MJ DeMarco

MJ DeMarco, in *The Millionaire Fastlane*, argues that the only dependable way to get rich is by owning your own business, specifically a business that offers a unique, valuable, and marketable product (either a commodity, for example, an appliance, or a service, such as programming). DeMarco argues that stocks are not dependable because of the threat of market crashes or the more mundane threat of a drop in stock values. Even retirement or other interest-bearing accounts are not dependable, again because of the threat of a market crash, and because of inflation which amounts to a loss of real worth ($3 million today may only be worth $1 in real value by the time you retire). Further, investing in a time-consuming and costly college degree will not only drain your financial resources but will give you a late start and will not give you the skills you need to be an adept business owner -- the skills of creativity, drive, and financial and consumer-market sense -- all of which you can learn on your own. In order to create a business that thrives without a focus on the "tried and true" those markets are already cornered and swamped with the competition. Instead, be inventive, focus on creating something new that will be in demand and meet customer needs. Finally, switch from a consumer to a business owner mindset. Examine products, advertisements and businesses through a "behind the scenes" lens, investigating their business and advertising model and the value and ingenuity of their product.

The Automatic Millionaire By David Bach

In his book, *The Automatic Millionaire*, David Bach explains how shifting to automatic savings, investments, and bill payments, as well as cutting down on small unnecessary expenses, can make you a millionaire by the time you retire. One key point made by this book -- a theme shared with Kiyosaki -- is the value of "paying yourself first". Most people pay their bills, taxes, and other expenses first and then (hopefully) save or (better) invest what is left over. However, this is backward: you should put money into your retirement fund, rainy day fund, savings, and investments first and then deal with your bills and expenses with the remainder. Automating these savings and investments will allow this process to become second nature and change this use of money from optional to non-negotiable. Putting a percentage of your income in your savings or retirement fund before your check is cut is also a great way to save money and reduce loss of income from taxes. Equally important to "paying yourself first" and automating savings and investments, is cutting down or eliminating unnecessary small costs, such as coffee or food out or other impulse buys can increase your expendable income (and therefore your savings and investments) drastically over the course of your working life.

The Wealthy Barber By David Chilton

David Chilton's *The Wealthy Barber,* is a financial guide told through a narrative lens. The story follows the main characters as they seek out and learn the wisdom of a barber who has become wealthy through financial conservation and literacy. A recurrent theme in the financial guides discussed in this chapter, the barber advises first and most importantly to "pay yourself first".

Deciding upon a meaningful, but manageable, amount of your income to set aside from each paycheck is the first step to "making your money work for you" (in the words of Kiyosaki). The barber suggests setting aside 10%—this amount is enough to build up and do something worthwhile with, but not so much that it will drastically change your lifestyle. However, building up extra cash alone will not make you a millionaire. To accomplish this goal, you have to make your money make you money, that is, you need to invest. The wealthy barber suggests putting your money into investments, like mutual funds, which, while they have a lower overall rate of return, are far more secure. The wealthy barber holds that pouring your money into stocks is essentially gambling. The wealthy barber also warns against putting your money into property or other assets that may take away from the money you are able to invest. Buying a home can provide a return if you play your cards right, but if paying your mortgage takes money out of your savings, it's a loss.

The Richest Man in Babylon By George Clason

In *The Richest Man in Babylon*, George Clason explains that the keys to accumulating wealth lie in a mindset focused on earning, saving, learning, and prudence. Clason uses pearls of wisdom from throughout history and the analogy of Babylon -- one of the richest civilizations -- to exemplify his points. Unlike many other books on cultivating a wealth-focused or "rich" mindset, Clason focuses, not on the investment side, but rather on the earning side. The key to accumulating wealth is in earning. The more you earn, the more you can save. Mastering your trade, and better, learning new trades, will expand your capacity to earn. You should also seek out advice, but make sure you are seeking out advice only from those who are financially knowledgeable and responsible. Because, as earning grows often, so does the cost of one's lifestyle, you need to maintain a simple lifestyle and save at least 10% of your earnings and use the rest for your expenses. Debt should be paid off as soon as reasonably possible -- if you are in debt 20% of your income should go to paying it off. However, while saving 10% and paying off debts, you should also not put so much money away or into debt that you deprive yourself. Adopt a frugal but reasonably comfortable lifestyle. Investing is wise if you are careful. Do not invest in ventures that do not offer a meaningful return or those that seem too good to be true.

Chapter 7: Invest like the Pros

You can follow the lead of investment professionals like Warren Buffett and Ray Dalio to succeed in the investing game and maximize your Money Machine. In this chapter, we offer insights on how to invest like these two giants of investment and finance, using public investment information from their companies.

7.1 Warren Buffett (Berkshire Hathaway)

Despite being a billionaire and one of the richest people in the world,

Buffett—also known as the Oracle of Omaha—is known for living in his modest Nebraska home and avoiding spending on luxury items, opting instead for a burger and Cherry Coke as a treat.

Famous as an ultra-long value investor, Buffett eschews the new in favour of time-tested classics, such as Coca-Cola, BNSF, GEICO, and See's Candies. One exception to this rule is Buffett's investment in tech giant, Apple, maker of the popular iPhone, as well as e-commerce retailer, Amazon.

Berkshire Hathaway, Buffett's company, holds a number of popular value investments in their portfolio besides the above-mentioned companies, including American

Express, Bank of America Corporation, Biogen, Costco, Davita Dialysis, General Motors Company, Johnson & Johnson, Procter & Gamble, UPS, and many other well-known, high-performing, and high-reputation companies.

7.2 Ray Dalio (Bridgewater)

Buffett's spendthrift nature sets him apart from other investors, like Ray Dalio, who owns Bridgewater Associates, an asset management firm and the world's largest hedge fund. Dalio, a graduate of Harvard Business School, wrote a 132-page volume on what helped him succeed in investing. Among these is the ability to accept and deal with the issues that one faces in life. Another is listening to others and maintaining good relationships with family and friends. While money can be fleeting, relationships can be more long-lasting. Using reality as a compass, Dalio believes, can help one succeed in the investment world. Risk management is also a very large part of this strategy.

Dalio's Bridgewater invests in Biogen (like Berkshire Hathaway), as well as pharmaceutical company Bristol-Myers Squibb Company, United Rentals, Macy's, steel producer Nucor Corporation, Royal Bank of Canada, Eastman Chemical Company, and Alliance Data Systems.

Chapter 8: Conclusions

"If you don't find a way to make money while you sleep, you will work until you die."
Warren Buffett

Investing can be overwhelming. It can feel like there's a lot of information to learn, a lot of math, and you may be intimidated by the typical image of the investor that you see—a professional working on the Wall Street floor. The truth is that anyone can get started in investing. By using the right strategies and doing your research, you can make sure that you make the most of your money machine.

Investing doesn't have to be difficult. Approach investing with a curious mind. Remain eager to learn. After following the markets for a while, making various mistakes and successes, following the news, etc., you will get a feel for how it all works. There is nothing that can substitute this type of experience, so be prepared for that, and have a growth and learning mindset.

Once again, congratulations on considering or deciding to pursue a dream that few people will experience first hand. Stay excited, curious and meticulous in learning all you can—once you take action daily for six months, it may change how you define yourself.

References

Bach, David. 2016. "The Automatic Millionaire (Expanded and Updated): A Powerful One-Step Plan to Live and Finish Rich." Crown Publishing Group: New York.

Chen, James. 2020. "Dividend Growth Rate." *Investopedia*. Retrieved September 27th, 2020. https://www.investopedia.com/terms/d/dividendgrowthrate.asp

Chen, James. 2020. "Basis Points (BPS)." *Investopedia.* Retrieved September 27th, 2020. https://www.investopedia.com/terms/b/basispoint.asp

Chilton, David. 1998. "The Wealthy Barber: Everyone's

Commonsense Guide to Becoming Financially Independent." Prima Publishing: Roseville, CA.

Clason, George. 2018 (1926). "The Richest Man in Babylon." Sound Wisdom: Shippensburg, PA.

Cothern, Lance. "What is the 50/30/20 rule budget?" *Credit Karma.* Retrieved September 27th, 2020. https://www.creditkarma.com/advice/i/50-30-20-rule

DeMarco, MJ. 2011. "The Millionaire Fastlane: Crack the Code to Wealth and Live Rich for a Lifetime!" Viperion Publishing Corporation: Phoenix.

Duggan, Wayne and John Divine. 2020. "The Complete Berkshire Hathaway Portfolio." *US News.* Retrieved September 27th,

2020.
https://money.usnews.com/investing/stock-market-news/slideshows/the-complete-berkshire-hathaway-portfolio?slide=45

Eker, T. Harv. 2005. "Secrets of the Millionaire Mind: Mastering the Inner Game of Wealth." HarperCollins Publishers: New York.

Hills, Napoleon. 2016 (1937). "Think and Grow Rich." The Ralston Society: Meriden, CT.

Kiyosaki, Robert T. 1997. "Rich Dad, Poor Dad: What the Rich Teach Their Kids About Money – That the Poor and Middle Class Do Not!" Warner Books: New York.

Kiyosaki, Robert T. 2011. "Rich Dad's Cashflow Quadrant: Guide to Financial Freedom." Warner Books: New York.

Questrade. Retrieved September 27th, 2020. https://www.questrade.com/home

Robinhood. Retrieved September 27th, 2020. https://robinhood.com/us/en/

Sincero, Jen. 2018. "You Are a Badass at Making Money: Master the Mindset of Wealth." Penguin Books: New York.

The Vanguard Group, Inc. "Don't let high costs eat away your returns." Retrieved September 27th, 2020. https://investor.vanguard.com/investing/how-to-invest/impact-of-costs

US Securities and Exchanges Commission. Office of Investor Education and Advocacy. "How

Fees and Expenses Affect Your Investment Portfolio." *Investor Bulletin*. Retrieved September 27th, 2020. https://www.sec.gov/investor/alerts/ib_fees_expenses.pdf

Wealthsimple. Retrieved September 27th, 2020. https://www.wealthsimple.com/en-us/

Wikipedia. "Compound interest." Retrieved September 27th, 2020. https://en.wikipedia.org/wiki/Compound_interest

Yochim, Dayana and Jonathan Todd. "How a 1% Fee Could Cost Millennials "590,000 in Retirement Savings." *nerdwallet.* Retrieved September 27th, 2020. https://www.nerdwallet.com/blo

g/investing/millennial-retirement-fees-one-percent-half-million-savings-impact/

Zitter, Leah. 2019. "How Did Ray Dalio Get Rich?" *Investopedia.* Retrieved September 27th, 2020. https://www.investopedia.com/articles/insights/072516/how-did-ray-dalio-get-rich.asp

Thank you for reading this book!

If you found this book helpful, I would be grateful if you would post an honest review on Amazon so this book can reach and help other people.

All you need to do is to visit

amazon.com/author/senseipauldavi d

click the correct book cover and click on the blue link next to the yellow stars that says, "customer reviews."

As always... It's a great day to be alive!

Check Out Another Book In This Series Visit:

www.amazon.com/author/senseipauldavid

Or

Search Amazon.com #senseipublishing

SENSEI
SELF DEVELOPMENT
B O O K S   S E R I E S
senseiselfdevelopment.senseipublishing.com

Sensei Paul David

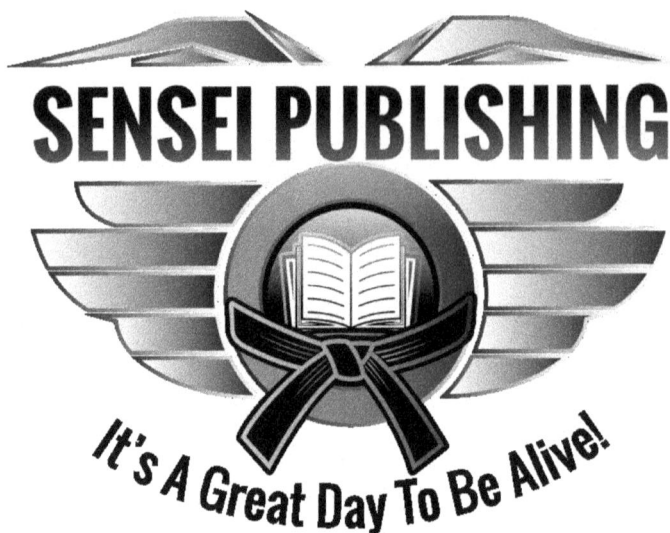

SENSEI PUBLISHING

It's A Great Day To Be Alive!

www.senseipublishing.com

@senseipublishing
#senseipublishing

Check out our **recommendations** for other books for adults & kids plus other great resources by visiting www.senseipublishing.com/resources/

Join Our Publishing Journey!

If you would like to receive FREE BOOKS, special offers, please visit www.senseipublishing.com and join our newsletter by entering your email address in the pop-up box, and

Follow Our Engaging Blog NOW!
senseipauldavid.ca

Get Our FREE Books Today!
Click & Share the Links Below

FREE Kids Books
lifeofbailey.senseipublishing.com
Kidsonearth.senseipublishing.com

FREE BONUS!!!
Experience Over 25 FREE Engaging Guided Meditations!

Prized Skills & Practices for Adults & Kids. Help Restore Deep-Sleep, Lower Stress, Improve Posture, Navigate Uncertainty & More.

Download the Free Insight Timer App and click the link below:

http://insig.ht/sensei_paul

If you like these meditations & want to go deeper email me for a FREE 30min LIVE Coaching Session:

senseipauldavid@senseipublishing

About the Author

I create simple & transformative eBooks & Guided Meditations for Adults & Children proven to help navigate uncertainty, solve niche problems & bring families closer together.

I'm a former finance project manager, private pilot, jiu-jitsu instructor, musician & former University of Toronto Fitness Trainer. I prefer a science-based approach to focus on these & other areas in my life to stay humble & hungry to evolve. I hope you enjoy my work and I'd love to hear your feedback.

- It's a great day to be alive!

Sensei Paul David

Facebook, Instagram, YouTube:
@senseipublishing

Scan using your phone/iPad camera for
Social Media
Visit us at www.senseipublishing.com
and sign up to our newsletter to learn
more about our exciting books and to
experience our FREE Guided
Meditations for Kids & Adults.

Follow/Like/Subscribe:

Facebook, Instagram, YouTube:

@senseipublishing